My Hero My Traitor:
The Edward Snowden Story

John Washington

ISBN-13: 978-0615946344
ISBN-10: 0615946348

www.CamiEyes.com

DEDICATION

Victims of Computer Hackers

CONTENTS

ACKNOWLEDGMENTS
The Staff of CamiEyes, Inc.
www.CamiEyes.com

CHAPTER ONE
HERO OR TRAITOR?

The National Security Agency(NSA) seems to be crumbling under the weight of the allegations made by their former contractor, Edward Snowden. Snowden is not your typical geek; though extremely talented in his trade, Snowden has proven himself to be an outspoken U.S. citizen who is concerned about the welfare of his fellow Americans and the world at large. Is he a hero or traitor?

Throughout his tenure at the NSA, Snowden frequently notified his superiors whenever he saw something was amiss and that the system was exposed to threats. His superiors duly recognized his efforts and accorded him with the privileges reserved for high ranking officials within the NSA.

Having at one time been subcontracted to cover for one of his superiors who was away on vacation, Snowden used this time to dig deep into the secrets surrounding NSA monitoring. The U.S government has been put squarely on the spot for the questionable activities that have been brought to light by Snowden.

The NSA is still trying to find out how much information is being held by Snowden and has not yet been released to the media. In his own words, Snowden values privacy and can't picture himself living in a society where every move, business transaction, instant message and conversation is recorded without the individual's knowledge and locked away forever. He is vehemently pushing for an end to the surveillance carried out by the NSA on all fronts. The NSA surveillance, according to the files leaked by Snowden, extends to Sao Paulo, Brazil. This powerful agency of the U.S government has massive resources and has already managed to put a huge proportion of the population under surveillance.

CHAPTER TWO
SURVEILLANCE VIOLATES HUMAN RIGHTS

Snowden fled imprisonment in the United States as a result of leaking NSA's secret surveillance files by seeking temporary asylum in Russia where he is currently residing. Though not frequent on television, Snowden has attended a few interviews and explained his actions to the whole world hoping for support. Things are working out for him as it is; Brazilian leaders recently requested him to testify in court as they press charges against NSA for reportedly tracking mobile phones within Sao Paulo. With permanent asylum beckoning, Snowden might evade arrest by the United Sates and continue exciting people to stand up against unwarranted surveillance by the U.S. government. His concerns are further fueled by the fact that the Constitution protects against unsubstantiated surveillance of an individual by any entity. Snowden has stated that the accusations he has leveled against the NSA are legitimate and protected by the Constitution.

Snowden is not just a wild fire abrasively setting all things in his way ablaze; his thoughts are calmly and decisively collected, a fact that has been widely acknowledged in the global community. As relayed by a colleague, Snowden received many accolades for his NSA work. During his time as a NSA contractor, his responsibilities and access steadily rose albeit in a short time. This won him many favors and as a result, he was granted access into virtually all of NSA's files. Being a decisive and critical minded individual, he began to questions information he read in top secret files. The rate at which surveillance by the NSA is growing was worrying, according to Snowden. He believes digitization is rapidly corroding the core of human rights in the U.S. The violation of human rights has now shifted to surveillance. Snowden believes the United States government will not let him go free so he is seeking permanent asylum in Brazil.

The Brazilian government has voiced its opinion and condemned these surveillances. Earlier in the year, reports that Brazil's President had her phone tapped into for surveillance ignited a strong response. The files leaked by Snowden revealed that many other world leaders had their phones tapped into by the NSA.

CHAPTER THREE
SNOWDEN ASYLUM IN RUSSIA

At Snowden's NSA workstation, he kept a copy of the United States Constitution; this shows the source for his arguments. He used the Constitution for reference purposes and to ensure that the NSA projects did not violate the Constitution. Up until now, Snowden's stance on his constitutional right to privacy has not been challenged. He still believes that the Constitution will confirm what he views as an abuse of power at the NSA.

Recently, District Court Judge Richard Leon in the state of Washington ruled that the activities being executed by the NSA in the name of enhancing security may be violating the Constitution. This appears to be a victory for Snowden. He views it as a timely decision which will prove that his actions were instinctively guided with a pure motivation to protect privacy rights protected by the United States Constitution. It has been stated in the media that he purportedly is working out a permanent asylum deal in Brazil from where he will be aiding the Brazilian government to counter surveillance tactics by foreign governments. Time will confirm whether this is true. Is he a hero or traitor?

CHAPTER FOUR
THE RELENTLESS STORM

Months after Snowden leaked highly classified files to the media, he has adopted a relatively private life away from the press. Snowden still seems to be passionate about his course to expose the activities of the NSA. It is assumed that he will get back into the limelight as soon as he is granted permanent asylum.

If Snowden succeeds in gaining asylum, we do not know what he will do with the remaining NSA files. The early leaks have already brewed a relentless storm and the public is now vigilant to know more about the top secret files and how else they might have been targeted by the NSA.

The fact that NSA is a government agency may mean that there is more to this mass surveillance than meets the eye; for one, Snowden is strongly convinced that the surveillance being carried out by the NSA has unacceptable motives. This former NSA contractor hopes to offer his skills again and address what he terms as gross human rights violations with technology.

His years in the NSA have been characterized by a bold and fearless spirit when it came to confronting occupational challenges. He almost lost his job after confronting a superior over the reprimand of a colleague; for him, human rights and dignity have to be upheld at whatever cost.

CHAPTER FIVE
TOP SECRET FILES

American citizens are realizing that surveillance by the NSA is not just reserved for actors in the movies; it is happening to real life people according to the top secret files leaked by Snowden. The leaked files also reveal that surveillance is being carried out on a wide scale and that it is getting more pervasive by the day. Snowden worries that if it is not halted immediately, there will no longer be such a thing as privacy.

The uncovering of this secret surveillance by the NSA has been termed by human rights activists led by

Snowden as a major undoing of constitutionally protected privacy.

CHAPTER SIX
NSA AMNESTY DEAL

It has been reported that the NSA has made it clear that it may partake in an amnesty deal with Snowden if he hands back the files that are still in his possession. Noncompliance with this might result in the NSA revoking an amnesty deal and the release of more incriminating files. As to whether Snowden will buy into this amnesty deal still remains to be seen. However, it has been clearly stated by the Attorney General that amnesty is not an option.

The uncertainty in these reports may be due to the unconfirmed report that Brazil may offer Snowden permanent asylum in exchange for his skills in unraveling computer systems dilemmas; using this knowledge, the country may be hoping that it will be able to lay a transatlantic cable and use internet servers based in Europe and other "friendly" countries and desist from relying on the United States. One of the key factors that has been deemed by experts as the chief initiator of the surveillance is the fact that U.S substantively participated in the building of the infrastructure for supporting high-speed transatlantic fiber optic cables.

As a way of preventing further intrusions into their classified and unclassified files, the NSA reportedly dismantled all the computers that Snowden used during his tenure at their premises and replaced them at a cost estimated to be in millions of dollars. Fearing that Snowden had infected the computers with viruses in order to continually gain access to top secret files, the NSA replaced the NSA workstations with new computer systems. The alleged ability that Snowden was able to hack into strong firewalls and access highly classified data leads one to believe that the NSA has a lot of evaluations to do with regards to the safety of their systems.

CHAPTER SEVEN
VIOLATION OF PRIVACY

As stated by District Court Judge Leon, the multiple NSA surveillance programs have not fulfilled their core mandate to date. Instead, they may be violating the constitutional protection to privacy. Having failed to prevent even a single terrorist attack since inception, these surveillance programs seem to be serving another purpose, that of spying on individuals in the U.S. and abroad.

The lack of supporting evidence to back NSA's claims only agitated the judge who duly questioned the government's involvement and adoption of these surveillance programs. This constitutional challenge will go down as an enthralling battle with analysts having predicted that the spirit and power enshrined in the U.S. Constitution will prevail. The metadata collection program method being carried on by the NSA is being viewed as a violation of privacy. It is argued that unless there are clear signs that an individual's behavior calls for an investigation, an individual should not be subjected to an unwarranted surveillance. Going by this, Snowden clearly knew that he would use the U.S. Constitution as defense for leaking the secret NSA files. However, another U.S. District Judge, William Pauley, in the state of New York stated within the last few days that the NSA phone surveillance is indeed legal under the Patriot Act. Is Edward Snowden a hero or a traitor?

CHAPTER EIGHT
U.S. PASSPORT REVOKED

In his early letter to the public, Snowden wrote that he would never be allowed to speak out freely by the U.S. Government due to an unraveling surveillance program being facilitated by the NSA. Fortunately or unfortunately for Snowden, the world seems to have taken his action as support including the temporary asylum he is currently appreciating in Russia.

Upon learning that Snowden was responsible for disseminating the top secret activities of the global NSA surveillance program to the media and public in general, Snowden received news that his passport had been revoked by the United States limiting his ability to travel and seek asylum. This quick revocation meant one thing; the U.S. Government was hot on his heels and moving quickly to bring him home to justice in order for him to take full responsibility for his illegal actions.

Snowden's illegal activities have resulted in him being detached from his family and friends and may have resulted in him forfeiting the full rights of U.S. citizenship.

CHAPTER NINE
BRAZILIAN PRESIDENT SURVEILLANCE

Snowden revealed that the Brazilian president was one of the world leaders whose phone had been monitored by the NSA. This has generated great concern by the Brazilian government with the leadership expressing their anger at this revelation. Snowden, having been responsible for releasing the leaks, is also consequently responsible for passively alerting the Brazilian president of the surveillance being carried out in her country. He thus has a new reputation in Brazil and could comfortably live in the country after being granted permanent asylum. In Brazil, he won't have to keep looking over his shoulder due to fear of capture.

It has been reported that Brazil has reached out to Snowden and requested that he testify against the NSA. It also has been reported that Snowden not only wants asylum in Brazil in exchange for testifying; he also wishes to lend his services to the Brazilian government which has already stated that it wants to end the transatlantic fiber cable connection to America. If this is true, this may be an opportunity for Snowden to get his life back on a new track while doing what he loves best. Again, time will tell whether these reports are actually true.

Snowden is a man with limited options as it is. He would be acting in his own best interest by securing a permanent asylum as soon as possible and living free of a daily fear of being return to the United States against his will. Brazil appears to be a viable destination for him right now and there is no reason as to why he should not live in Brazil if granted permanent asylum. Is Snowden a hero or traitor?

CHAPTER TEN
THE SNOWDEN STORY

There is no telling as to where Snowden will end up or how his actions will impact the NSA and the U.S Government at large. So far, Snowden continues to live a private life and enjoys his temporary asylum in Russia while it lasts. He has shown that he is determined to acquire permanent asylum somewhere. Judging from his actions, he did not leak the files without a clear cut goal; a goal which he has achieved and continues to pursue further. The NSA on the other hand shows no intention of letting him go off easily. His actions have had far reaching implications and the individuals hardest hit won't stop until they bring him to justice. It's like a thriller, arousing more attention by the minute.

Right from the time he leaked the top secret NSA files, he has shown no regret and believes that his actions were aimed at revealing what he terms as atrocities committed by the NSA. His actions were somewhat supported by District Court Judge Leon who ruled that the surveillance being carried out by the NSA might be in violation of the United States Constitution. Snowden has been seen in public a few times in Moscow and it appears that he prefers to keep his many thoughts to himself until he is granted permanent asylum in his country of choice. Should Brazil grant him the asylum? Snowden may continue to leak top secret NSA files and discredit the surveillance programs being carried out by the NSA. It appears the files leaked from the NSA have not all been fully accounted for even after months of investigation. It has been reported that allegedly the NSA has set a very high bar for Snowden if he is to be granted amnesty. This includes the return of all the NSA files still in his possession. They worry that Snowden might release them to the media even after granting him the amnesty he had sought. With the option of waiting for the outcome of the debate on his amnesty or aggressively seeking permanent asylum, Snowden has shown that he is a free spirit exploring all the avenues available for his own survival.

The files that are still in the possession of Snowden might have details on the rest of the world leaders being monitored by the NSA; this may be one of the reasons as to why the U.S Government is cautious on the way it is handling the case. Snowden is being viewed as a modern day human rights crusader by some. The world has rapidly become centralized due to the advancements in technology and human rights are being violated through this same technology. As the Snowden story develops, we will keep you posted and offer insights to what is happening.

Is Snowden a hero or traitor? You decide. Join the debate at www.facebook.com/MyHeroMyTraitor.

WWW.CAMIEYES.COM

Made in the USA
Monee, IL
04 November 2026

67384400R00022